As We Cover Ourselves With Light

poems

Sandra Rivers-Gill

Sheila-Na-Gig Editions

Acknowledgments

This book was a labor of love and God's favor. It is with appreciation to Valerie King, Dianne Borsenik, Leah Leaderman, and those who have encouraged me in significant ways along my journey. A few poems in this book were generated in Tim Geiger's creative writing class and in the One-A-Day generative writing group curated by Jonie McIntire. A heartfelt gratitude to Hayley Mitchell Haugen at Sheila-Na-Gig Editions for embracing this book and my voice.

With humble gratefulness I wish to acknowledge the following editors of these fine journals who have given my poems a home, some in altered forms:

As It Ought To Be Magazine: "A Distant Hymn"
Common Threads: "Bon Voyage," "Fat Meat Is Greasy," "I'm Trying"
Flights Literary Magazine: "The River"
Hope Springs Eternal Anthology (Simple Simon Press): "Another Attempt to Make Hard-Boiled Eggs"
Jerry Jazz Musician: "Drummer"
Mock Turtle Zine: "In the Garden"
North of Oxford: "Conversation With My Great-Grandfather"
ONE ART: a journal of poetry: "D'Anjou"
redrosethorns magazine: "Ain't Nothing Like Family"
Rise Up Review: "Formal Education"

For my Mother

In Memory of Hattie Reed, my grandmother,
Mary Barrow, my great-grandmother,
and Fred Williams, Jr., my father.

Reading is important—read between the lines.
Don't swallow everything.

— Gwendolyn Brooks

Contents

Ain't Nothing Like Family

At the table we plant our hips,
spread roots deep into the soil,
gather and grow bony plates
from country fried chatter.

Something good
is always cooking.

The gospel of generous dessert
spoons our appetites
heaped all over hallelujahs.

It tests our mettle,
stirs up a season of wait;

gives us a bold flavor to chew.
We ask for second helpings,
because we thirst for more
than pot liquor and cornbread.

Family is like leftover stew,
hearty as God's honest truth.
It's what Mama places on the table.

Before our prayers rise up
we come together—

churn homemade ice cream.
We are a culture of ripened fruit
consuming what is not always easy.
We learn to appreciate our fullness—
savor our sweet and spice.

On our tongues we crave living water;
well done like ribs on a summer grill
perfected in the smoke of fire.

We are marinated in love,
seasoned with salt for our journey.

Conversation With My Great-Grandfather

—from a photograph, 1935

Perhaps you own only this Fedora—
black-brimmed to halo your head below;
a nod angled up from jawlines,
high as distant mountains.

I see you are unaware of me
probing a past I want to know.
Your game-face, is it not shocked
by the eye of Kodak's close up?

Some might blink in a camera's burst
but you exude a shine from your surface,
shaded by a hat that does not pose
an opinion about being in this photo.

I am told you are an unread book.
Here, you are refined in sepia brown,
wearing a white open-collar
squinting from the lapel of your dark suit.

Is it unfashionable to smile?
Your clean-shave leaves a thin stash.
Full lips hum a silent note,
only you know the song.

The subtlety of your corners curl
as if you want to say, *Hello.*
Tip your hat—
properly introduce yourself.

Colored Imagination

—after Langston Hughes' "I Dream a World"

For my daughter

If a girl wants to braid her narrative,
let her dream a world with brown hands;
unshade the teacher's eyes—
caught her coloring outside the lines.

If brown hands are free to dream a world
they can discover boundless palettes
and color outside the line of
tones, textures, and trammels.

If a girl discovers unbound palettes
she can unlock the learning her mother offers
about tones, textures, and trammels—
how to hew meaning from rote memory.

If a girl's mother releases the learning,
her daughter will picture her own swirling sun
taking shape with meaning and new memory
from choices in her Crayola box.

If a girl imagines a swirling sun,
she can draw her shine across blank paper
with the crayons she chooses to use.
But the teacher will call her mother,

If a girl sparkles across white paper.
Does she have to return to school,
listen to the teacher talk about color,
how the girl mixed them up?

If she goes back to school with her mother
the girl will show the teacher her sun—
how she mixed every color in the box
beyond the boundary of her desk.

If a girl teaches the teacher about her sun
colored from the world of her brown hands,
beyond the margin of a grammar school desk,
the girl will weave her own narrative.

She Watches From Her Booth

We fill ourselves with a bouquet that savors
the sweet honeycomb of dessert.

He settles the check—
I place my hand in his.

On our way out
we pass through low-lit patrons—
table scraps of conversation.

My hair is a beehive—
a frohawk of buzz.
His fitted cap covers
a blond anthem of blue eyes.

Our skin unforgettable in chiaroscuro light.

We slip by a sounding booth.
The silver of a woman's tongue
is tied and heaped on her plate.

Her spoon is a pause in midair.

Snip

It is how the barber begins
to censor a man.

He can no longer comb over
but cut the thin that lingers.

Not too much off!
The man protests.

His tuft clouds
tumble to the floor.

Fists unfurling the fight.

This Bathing Seat

holds the weight of gravity
where dimpled cheeks sit heavy
and feet wade in balmy water; where
she questions the coolness climbing
into this room of sweltering weather;
where her silver strands cling to her
shoulders—damp with memory.
Her private spa has a mind to flux and foam
and flow down her back flesh; only
one breast glistens—the other given
to mastectomy; where she planted
a patch of patience before the stroke
and ceded herself to us; where life has
loosened her; where our hands hold
the thick skin folded in her lap; where
everything is bathed, and she trusts
this pampering; where her body bares
its secrets.

I'm Trying

She stops by unexpectedly,
but the light of her smile warms me.

Her bodily frame arcs like a teapot spout.
The brew of her day pours into our home.

She and I used to see eye to eye. Now gravity
bends her spine to the south inches less than mine.

Is it true that as one grows in wisdom,
one's physical stature decreases in volume?

Is this a place where dreams cannot be accessed?
Scratch my back, she will say. *I cannot reach the spot.*

It is an elusive place. *But something is there.*
I raise her shirt to see what it is, gently scratch

the raised age spots. That span of her back
appears as an exploding constellation of stars.

I stand there to gaze at them shooting,
their flares drifting across her back,

guess at the galaxy she is describing.
But I am a million miles away from easing her itch.

A Distant Hymn

He owns a pre-loved sedan
the shade of passive beige—
not at all rebellious or disrespectful.

The four of us push open a dream,
a distant hymn to buckle into.
Our journey is a shifting map.

On Sundays the car sits in the drive,
stores up empty praises,
fills a collection plate of dim memory.

I never heard a preacher's faux sermon
given from the pulpit of a couch—
nor mumbling words from keys
he keeps in his pocket.

The three of us march on
wearing the rain of broken umbrellas.

Family Tree

We learn to rise—
place our distinctive sound
on the bough of our song.

Our name rustles
a legacy we leave behind.

What feeds our soul
though we may break,

we emerge,
deep-rooted in resilience.

How Ends Meet

—for my grandmother

Daddy's hands could dance and hunt wild rabbit
stew to fill our plates. Grateful for *Amazing Grace*.
When winters cawed like crows, daddy sacrificed
his new shoes to measure a shifting of our small feet.
He drove his own feet into rubber car tires found
at the edge of dusty roads in Opelika. Eased us into fine
leather boots. With fortitude laced up our legs, we
stood outside the white man's business. They say daddy
was unskilled, but he labored on broken bridges
to erect a humble home for us. Fueled our old wood
stove with his bright flame. Mama sewed my sisters and me
into flour sack dresses. Fashioned our seams into
a curtsied life in Jesus' name. She took in white folks' dirty
laundry and boarders that blessed the budget. Meager
was a price paid for a piece of fat pork to boil in
a season of drought. When brown gravy stirred
a recession, it was proof that a little milled flour,
baking soda, and hot water could make Johnnycakes
butter our bellies. Mama preserved what daddy provided.
She could peel the fur from peaches, curl her wrist and
pick from dark vines; blackberries so sweet,
she cooked them to a slow jam on Saturday nights.

What I Remember About My Great-Grandmother

how *Baby*
loosed her lips.
my first name

hushed into
yesterday
but found me

everyday.
after school
the lessons.

***

tucked inside
cheek and gum,
her fancy

peach tree twig.
sweet-dipped chew
spat her sound

in a jar.
juice flowed foul
from my hands.

***

she taught me
moments will
make bookmarks.

every page
will turn time.
she spent it

listening
to His voice—
small and still

***

she praised God
on brewed morns
with biscuits.

sprung up to
free her mind
from thin threads;

silver plaits,
dark days and
memory

***

her vestige—
backbone and
weary soles.

slow dances
rise and fall
on hardwood.

I still hear
her carved cane
tapping tunes.

Marvel

He toddles from my reach to uncontested territory.
His flannel blanket, a cape billowing behind. His
fast feet propel him to leap from indifferent surfaces
onto a level floor. The land of freedom calls his name.
Around the house light shifts shadow into scary shapes
propped against a barrier of walls. He runs. I tell him
the sun will always expose tricks that frighten him.
And he kicks a ball freely to the net of his desired goal.
This small boy's body thunders, bicycles his legs
in the air of victory. Like Pele. He collects a creed
in himself. Carries power in his worth. His vision is
a beacon of hope passed down by the ancestors. He has
conquered landscapes he wants to love. Finds safe passage
back to me. Says he is a superhero. I believe him.

Pressed

—*circa 1970s*

Her hair tightened up to defend itself
following a fistful of revolt.

In the kitchen the hot comb hisses
a soulful hallelujah.

As blue pomade fell like anointing,
each strand bounced forth from dry bones; quenched.

When whirlwinds sought to steal her praise
she found a song to shape her journey.

In the relentless rain her pressed curls prevailed
beneath a canopy of ribs that sprung up like faith.

Her slender hands churched into prayer,
shifted from old refrains to hymns.

They did not see her coal black crown
flipping a frame around her shine.

Between the Lines

It's seven a.m..
Moments unfold
the pages of my book.
It is my rise and shine,

my teatime turns
to task time.

My mother phones me.
Our cousin is driving to town.

She has forgotten.
He called yesterday,
Now on his way with his new wife.

I hear her familiar refrain—
Wish I could make that casserole.

And I take on the task.
Her wish is a classic song
constantly playing in my head.

We have often sung
this popular standard.
The ask without asking—

masters it like a chef.
She stirs ideas
and cooks in absentia.

I adjust the volume
of her wistful sigh.
Tell her I will make

her favorite casserole.
It does not call for her hand.

She does not invite my help
but teaches me time and timbre—
the fine art of reading.

Between unspoken lines
mothers and daughters dwell.
We drive in our preferred lane,
sometimes cross the lines.

My mother forgets.

Sometimes I forget
how to plan a menu
on short notice.

In her mind
she will create the entire meal.
I will multitask by calculating the
time it takes to dress, shop, and bake—
deliver hospitality.

On the phone my mother sings,
Let us break bread together.

I say, *I will be there.*

She anticipates my role—
a gatherer of recipes,
and my place at the table,
enjoying a meal she has made.

Another Attempt to Make Hard-Boiled Eggs

When they say boil,
I think what they mean is
trouble the water.
Dress the black pot in sweat
and wild waves.

I place two raw eggs
in a small river of water.
Below the surface tension
I hear them wade and whistle;
trial and error.

So many eggs have I cracked.
This acquired taste is a seasoned dash,
a hardened meal worth
making a dish different—
no matter the cost.

Sometimes the shell wants to cling to
its own skin. I peel the fine flakes—
wash away the residue. Still
it holds to what it knows
nothing of letting go.

I repeat the process.
To be submerged is to be changed
by what is unseen before breaking.
It isn't a cliché that a watched pot never boils.
I have witnessed this timed truth
turn over again.

Eggs can be heated beyond
the hot burst of pressure.
It matters what is placed on the tongue.
It matters how it is prepared to be served.

At the Bureau of Motor Vehicles

I stand in the face of the machine,
a box with side blinders.

Pushed against my forehead
is a system of judgement,
a trick of tests.

I cannot fake the measure of blurs
betraying my honest effort to see
what I think is there.

Can't you read what you see?

The agent's sound is the shade of rude
reaching across a public service counter.

You are not quite accurate.

She raises a red flag for my failure.
My imperfect interpretation
are letters fading into the fringe.

Inside the box, I guess.
I blink for a miracle.

Narcolepsy

—for Mom

she is like a little red car racing towards disruption—
a detour of caution, blinking eyes anywhere; still
she searches for a perfect roundabout, a remedy
of sweet relief, pushes past endless roadblocks,
retreats in alleys that steer her absent from us;
she will deter the thief who rambles her words,
who lowers her lids, tucks her into slumber. he will
steal her flow but not her faith as she fights the pull
of evening shade rushing the sleep from her eyes.
she resides in unknown etiologies,

dreams of sheep;

too many to count.

Distance Is a Heavy Rope

My father tugs a long rope separating him and us.
Our red sled crackles across the shimmery streets
of Christmas stringing joy from home to home,
making magic of a moonless night. My father catches
himself after a slip of gravity. His gloved hands are battling
to keep their grip in the cold, but lets love slide around
an icy curve. I hear his thump-splash ahead of us;
his work boots an unfair rhythm, the blues of our laughter.
My brother and I pray before eavesdropped skies to
give in. *One more time,* we shout in the wake of falling
snow. Our knitted heads bobble for a taste of permanence
on our parched tongues. *This is the last time,* he shouts.
His fatigued shoulders and long legs whisk us around
another wintry block in the thin air of uncertainty. Nothing
shakes the inner chill. The distance between us
is my father's heavy footsteps frozen in time and swallowed
by memory. Only the stars offer their light.

Cancer

—the elephant in the room

After he pulls up the comfort of a brave front,
I see his smile in a blanket of pain.

He tells me his appetite is making a comeback.
I want to query the tumors clamoring for his attention

but he does not hear the weight of my concern.
Why is a calorie he will not count, the times

we have not sat in seats of conversation
to leave a trail of crumbs to discover later.

His sluggish bowels profit him nothing
but the company of our familiar headlines.

Prayer, strong coffee, and hospital Jell-O shots
allow him to consume what he can stomach.

The picking and prodding of unasked questions
have been long-playing tracks.

I offer a beloved verse before his meal.
We wait for our words to be served.

Stained Glass Windows
—for Dale

blossoms blush
altar bathed
in hued light

erasing
old notions
of loving

unbridled
tux and tulle
jump the broom

Crunching Numbers
—for Randy

When were we ever not counting?
It's one thousand miles;
ten hours if flying Lufthansa.

The back and forth of time zones;
we anticipate the familiar soil of reunions.

Between us, there are nineteen months.
We raise our voices like foreign flags,
hold conversations of countless journeys.

There are forty-two years to be translated
to remember the gulf of who we were.

We cannot talk about perceived distances
until we calculate what is missing.

Every Tub Has to Sit on Its Own Bottom

We were young when trouble found us
lying from the mouth of rebellion.

The truth was long, strict, and narrow—
grew from the boughs of wisdom.

It is there I studied accountability
from an abundance of backyard choices

As if hardheaded math could be broken down
into a prophetic rhythm of the *Watusi*.

In church they call it a holy dance;
legs filled with the spirit shut up in my bones;

arms waving the highest praise.

The Cardigan

My mother wears a frayed Sunday morning
as the sun streams through the pane
of her tears. The scent of heaven is weaved
into a sweater my grandmother's hands have
folded away. Inside this sweet solace,
birdsong mends her heart undone by memory.
Her mother's passing has emptied a wardrobe
of secondhand hugs and handwritten notes,
stained with rich recipes tucked into
warm pockets of conversations.
She wants to restore those tender threads,
but some buttons have gone missing.

What's in a Name?

—for Mary Charles Reed

When they say her name,
her sound does not return a grave.

She is present—
a belle-shaped muscle memory
in the mouths of old Southerners.

Her middle name is not a monument
erected to any man she has ever known.

The flow of her gospel is a kindling
shut up in her bones.

She is a train traveling north,
leaving the crow's dust behind
to spread its own shame.

The River

I've seen souls rise and fall like waves,
Ready for passage of drifting song.
I see cannulas traveling my father's face,
Like the Nile swimming upward, fighting gravity,
Against writhing and shedding of his Sunday suit.
He will leave behind a gaunt cocoon,
Echoing deferred reveries still thirsty.
We are children who follow the stars.
I am a child who wonders why
He and I never climbed those mountains.
I am witness to the conspicuously sharp
Cheekbone following a thin shadow of man.
His ashen hair curled tight as Ali's fists,
Determined to win the battle.
But lost time is dead weight, and it spreads its will
The way thorns push through unsown terrain.
I tell my Father I love him, and he turns his head
Toward the sound of my voice.
I pull a blanket over his unmasked shoulders,
And a sterile coolness envelopes the room.
There is no escaping his hoarse voice
Chased by jolting discomfort.
His eyes are engaged far beyond me,
Far beyond our distance
It is that deep gulf.
Neither of us found time to swim.
His eyes dip like two buoys
In unexplored rivers.

Uncovered

She found a secret yawning in the closet.
Its wings flapping in the ceiling
of rafters baring his shiny chicks.
They have never denied a looker.
So many spines pressed into his hands,
dog-eared to return to later.

She raised the pitched roof—
made her aria known.
The ring of a mezzo soprano
packed up the shit of antiquity
and feathered ambitions,
shooed the flighty birds into the light.

Blue Leather Gloves

She loves how they insulate
but do not slip on
inclement memory.

Carries them clutched,
casually, in one hand.
A styling trick.

Her husband once
called her *big-boned.*
But she is bold.

Holds a certain aesthetic—
the art of bare skin
touching the blues.

Her daughter says it's cold outside.
She replies, *I am fine.*
This is something she does.

Carrying on trends
will not keep her warm.
It is a reminder—

those past tense days.
Still, she holds their perfect fit.
Squeezes the leather like lemons.

Fat Meat Is Greasy

The air in our home spat like fat meat in a cast iron skillet.
It was as hot as the R & B hit, "Let's Stay Together,"
because love is supposed to taste better at home. Cooking
is what my mother did. *Money don't grow on trees*, she said.
The kitchen is where a family eats. It is where hard conversations
remain; where uneaten leftovers are served the next day for breakfast.
I remember a homemade hamburger sat waiting between slices
of Wonder Bread. My mother declared the dinner bell
had already struck, as my father's fire seasoned the kitchen with
piss on it greasing his lips. The front door slammed behind him.
My mother's clenched fist stirred across our secondhand table
to tenderize his vacancy. His sandwich oozed ketchup, cheese,
and tomato like tears. My young brother and I giggled at the gesture
of something we did not understand. The aroma of questions
lingered in the air.

In the Garden

From the road, at the edge of the driveway
the impatiens pose above the ground

Blooming like spring again in mid-July
until the mauve petals fall into the red mulch

She sees him kneeling in the resilient earth
next to dwarf roses who pout their peachy lips

They are willing to be plucked;
wine-hued petals, sinewy and blushing.

Their sweet scent appeals to confident bees
who enjoy the botanicals he has planted.

He quenches their thirst every evening,
controls wildflowers with his farmer-tanned hands

The way they reach and blossom into the sun;
he takes pride in pruning their silhouette.

He feeds the seed of a tomato taking root
as it ripens in the midst of Summer's splendor.

Patriarch

—for grandpapa

It is the improvised jam sessions—
the vocal remedy of melodies

flowing from your mouth,
a river rowing our little boats ashore.

You anchored us in cool expressions.
The staccato jazz of your twaddle notes

Ah-ah-ah-ah-ah convened from the pew
of your tongue.

An up-front man after the balm of Gilead,
you sang from the instrument of your lineage.

Ella would have been pleased
to have scatted on a stage with you

Ah-ah-ah-ah-ah-ah!
The read text of your gospel

a meeting tent perfectly pitched—
picnics spreading across our laps.

Call and Response

On a flatbed of summer he moved his harvest—
a spectacle of pole beans, sweet corn
and mustard greens. Stacked currency.
A farmer's field turned up on our city street.
His voice, a straining sound of timber
shouting and peddling his perishables
from a slim window of rising heat.
With idle curiosity a brother and sister
peek from the breach of a door. Playfully
replying in tandem, *Vegetable man!*
Inching wheels halted in front of our house;
eyes searching to see no one stirring.

Formal Education

My son informs me
he was schooled today.
Almost chalked up
like a blackboard lesson.

I am reminded
my son is a tree
bearing the danger
of low fruit suspended.

History is a class of teachers
marking him absent.
But he sees the chariots of fire.

My son tells me
he does not resist
the distant sound of
blue night calling him.

His answers attempt
to soothe the silence
in the trick of whirling lights.

He is a man.
No longer a boy
bound to dim narratives.
His truth is a false arrest.
The dog tags of discharge
hang about his neck.

My son tells me,
his life is a virtual classroom
full of routine exams

while onlookers
passively grade on curves
and theories
and metaphors
that detain a body.

His Song

steers a one-ton truck,
shifts gears
from work to rhythm

as he swerves to handle a highway.
his lips ring with clouds,
fling refrains from the window.

his arms wave in the breeze
as the riff of the road
changes lanes.

he turns up his anthem
like a rock star
thumping at traffic stops.

the rumble of his engine
enters the driveway—
home.

his hands key the door—
and sound spills open
like a concert.

D'Anjou

—for George Floyd

I had forgotten its coolness I carry
from ice box to counter slab.

A pear's taste is a hot commodity,
crisp and sweet.
Its body bares a certified label—
the inspector's choice.

Its unbroken skin sits silent
on my countertop.

The greenish-gold of its silhouette
does not wobble or
collapse like a cracked egg.

Funny how present tense
can worm its way into a memory.

When I was a young girl,
the white woman next door grew pear trees—
littered the ground with their fruit.

I had forgotten.
By summer's end she donned a straw hat,
climbed the ladder to her constellation of crops,
shared them with my brother and me.
The pears sat in our kitchen windowsill.
Our noses pressed against the scent
till they were ripe enough.

Now I stand at my kitchen counter
paring the skin from its flesh.
Its fresh tears stream in my hands.

I had forgotten pears ripen
at room temperature,
in their cultural climate.

I remember the instructions
that guarantee a pear's ripeness:
simply press its neck.

Bon Voyage

—for Fred

We are foreigners
far from understanding
each other's translation.

Our time zones
are separate countries
bordered by un-sailed seas.

We lack the luxury
of frequent flyer miles—
conversations not booked.

The keepsake of unsaid words
is the progression of long distance.

A second language
greeted us unexpectedly—
the love of letting go.

Drummer

He be funk and blues
and bebop. Scat!
Drops his shoes in cool.

His syncopated beat
flows free as pick-up sticks;
flies over the rim
of double-stroked rolls.

He got chops.

He got solos tappin',
a pulse pusher of lightnin' strikes.

His Hi-hats be raisin' the roof
of acoustical ocean waves.

He be an open mic,
a long distant hallelujah.

Epiphany

I remember your *aha* moment
when an uninvited guest took up residence
in your home and left a calling card.

Inside your left breast was an aggressive plot,
a landmine fastened to your life—
determined to be buried with your body.

But you are a contour map of calculated curves;
walking with faith across deep-rooted rivers,
looking for turned-up miracles.

The power of frequency is evident.
You trust the surgeon. His instrument of choice
broke into your beautiful skin.

He dismantled the bomb ticking like a clock,
and you are a warrior exploring her own atlas
carved into your chest of new memories.

You wear a full-fitted dress
because a flattened spirit never suited you
nor the carriage of imperfect cleavage.

When mom said Hugh Hefner was hiring,
cottontails bounced in your mood,
and you laughed in the face of eighty,

knowing you'd never pose for *Playboy*
though the thought gave you pause.
Your shine kept your pages turning.

She Sees Change

Buried in what is broken,
she bends her needs into a prayer.
Raises coins like Lazarus.

With steadfast hands
she recovers what has surrendered
to sundered sidewalks—

Bags a bargain
in the basement of her purse
just to balance a budget.

She teaches her children
how to shake off the dust;

how to resurrect something
from nothing.

The Quilt Maker

Holds the precision of skilled intention.
Unbroken, she threads our narrative.

It is the grace and sacrifice that gives comfort;
a vision of what she sews.

Because her prayers cut like shears,
she uses them as sowing instruments.

The eye is a long, sharp needle,
the intricacy of her fine hand work.

Home is where edges are salvaged—
eases us into shapes of steadfast faith.

It is the heat that presses open our minds—
gives texture to our embroidered roots.

To darn the most difficult fabric
is to unify our tough skin.

Pulling endurance from biased places,
she stretches us beyond its cotton presence.

The use of a thimble is a lost art form,
a safeguard from every human notion.

She eagerly gives insight to that which we
make into moments

as we cover ourselves with her light.

As I Drive By

I see her little green house still standing,
Hugged by good neighbors.

Her Granny Smith smile is heavenly,
Sweet as her deep-dish apple cobbler.

All she touched turned to dough
Rolled out in the garden of her kitchen.

She cooked double blooms rising,
Unmeasured her hands to scatter love.

The fragrance of her favorite recipes
Lingers in the rafters.

All of it passed on to us.

Every need met.
Every memory fully ripened.

About the Author

Sandra Rivers-Gill is a teaching artist. Her poetry is informed by family, community, and injustices, appearing in print journals, online and in anthologies while garnering numerous awards, including a nomination for Best of the Net. She is editor of *Dopeless Hope Fiends*, a book of poetry written by women in recovery. *As We Cover Ourselves With Light* is her first poetry collection. She resides in Toledo, Ohio, with her devoted husband, where she writes and is a caregiver, prayer, scrap art maker, poetry shopper, and when time allows, a performer in film or commercials.

Sheila-Na-Gig Editions